1. Introduction

Blue plaques have been used as historical markers for over 150 years to commemorate the lives of 'well-known' people and events or to relate the significance of certain buildings, past and present.

The first blue plaque scheme was set up in London in 1866. The scheme was inspired by British politician William Ewart (1798-1869) who proposed to the House of Commons in 1863 that famous people and events should be commemorated with plaques. The idea was adopted by the Society of Arts in 1866 with the first plaque being erected in 1867. This first plaque commemorated the life of Romantic poet Lord Byron (1788-1824) but the house on which the plaque was placed was demolished in 1889 and the plaque was lost. However, other plaques had been erected in the interval and the scheme continues today. In 1901, London Council (later Greater London Council) took over the scheme and ran it until 1986.

Since 1986, the London scheme has been run by English Heritage. Apart from a brief attempt to roll the scheme out nationally from 1998 to 2005, the focus of the scheme has been the greater London area.

Since this London scheme was set up, other blue plaque schemes have followed. Many have adopted the style of the London plaques with white lettering on a blue background and the idea of using circular plaques has also been copied. However, not all 'blue plaques' are blue – some schemes use different colours – and not all are round – some use different shapes. And while the London 'official' plaques are ceramic and usually embedded into the wall of the buildings to which they are affixed, other schemes use other materials – often, but not exclusively, metal.

Here in Wakefield, the first plaques to be erected came in 1988 when, following an initiative by the local authority's Tourism Officer, Chantry Rotary sponsored one on Wakefield Bridge and a second one was placed at the site of the former Mines Rescue Station in Ings Road.

2. Wakefield Civic Society Blue Plaque Scheme

Wakefield Civic Society started is own blue plaque scheme in 1995.

In that year, a grant from the National Lottery was obtained and this enabled 10 blue plaques to be erected in and around the city centre. In 2000, the Society successfully applied for a Millennium Lottery grant and this led to a further 12 plaques being added to the Society's collection. In 2004, as part of a project to commemorate the Society's 40th birthday, a further 4 plaques were commissioned (and actually erected in 2005) and more plaques followed in response to nominations from Society members and members of the public.

In 2005, with funding from Wakefield *first*, the Development Agency for Wakefield at the time, the Society published 3,000 copies of our first *Blue Plaque Trail*. This contained details of the 30 blue plaques we had in our collection at the time. The book was used as the basis for talks and guided walks and the booklets were all given away. The booklet contained text prepared by Kate Taylor working with me and with input from John Goodchild.

By 2011, the number of blue plaques in the Society's collection had grown again, albeit only to 32, and it was time for a new booklet, so a second edition was published with updated photos and revised text, again by Kate Taylor and me, with additional help from John Goodchild. The booklet was designed for us by Wakefield Council's in-house Design and Print Service and 3,000 copies were ordered. In fact, the printing company accidentally printed an extra 3,000 copies, which we agreed to buy at cost, so we found ourselves in possession of some 6,000 copies – which came in a great many boxes! While we continued to give away copies to members and at special events, and also made some available on request to schoolteachers and others for their projects, we also offered copies for sale in an attempt to recover some of the cost of printing the booklet.

Over the years, the stock of the 2011 edition has dwindled and it is time to produce a new guide to the Society's blue plaques – and this brings us to the book you are now reading.

This new book brings us right up to date and features all 61 blue plaques in the Society's collection. The larger format of this book compared with the earlier booklets means that there is more space for text and images. Sadly, with the passing of both Kate Taylor and John Goodchild since the earlier versions were published, I have had no experts to turn to for the text so, while some of the words from the original publications have found their way into this new edition, the expanded text – and new text for the blue plaques we have erected since 2011 – is down to me.

I have relied on my growing library of books on local history and internet-based research to provide this expanded text (and must take full responsibility for any errors of fact). While there are too many books to cite individual sources for all facts, where I have relied particularly on one or more sources for individual entries, I have provided endnotes on page 47 showing the original sources to enable further reading should you wish to pursue your own research.

Since the Society instigated its blue plaque scheme in 1995, most of the plaques have been erected as a result of external funding, often by way of donations from individuals and organisations. Throughout the book, the sources of the external funding have been indicated and I wish to put on record the Society's thanks to all who have contributed so generously.

Without this funding, our blue plaque collection would be just a fraction of what it is today. For entries where no funding source is given, the plaque has been paid for out of the Society's own funds.

2016: Gill Sykes and Elsie Walton unveiling the plaque for East Lodge.

2015: Kate Taylor with the plaque to Constance Heward

2017: The Mayor of Wakefield, Cllr Kevin Barker with Matthew and Jenny Burton of Qubana, 1-3 Wood Street

2022: Unveiling the plaque for Fanny Stott - David and Eleanor Woollin with the author (centre) and the Mayor and Mayoress of Wakefield: Cllr David Jones and Mrs Annette Jones. Photo by Shaun Walker.

3.   Our Blue Plaque Collection

The Society's plaques are spread far and wide around the city centre and further afield so, rather than trying to arrange them as one complete walking tour as we did in the earlier booklets, for this new publication, the plaques are arranged around four separate trails – the Northgate Trail, the Wood Street Trail, the Westgate Trail and the Kirkgate Trail – and a map is provided for each. This will enable the enthusiast who wishes to explore the city centre plaques on foot to divide their effort over a number of walks rather than trying to do them all at once. Even with this arrangement, however, there are still a number of plaques way beyond the city centre for which you will needs wheels and possibly a compass to explore.

I should point out that only the blue plaques erected solely by the Society are covered in this book (the ones that have the Society's name at the top). Plaques erected by others are not included and this includes those the Society worked on in partnership with Dream Time Creative under the Forgotten Women of Wakefield project.

Please bear in mind that, from time to time, we may have to remove plaques for refurbishment or re-wording when new facts are uncovered or a building is modified or its use changed. The text and illustrations in this new book can, therefore, only be seen as a snapshot of what exists at the time of writing.

This is not the end of the story, however. We have new plaques already in the pipeline and a long list of nominations yet to work through. We will, without doubt, going on adding to our blue plaque collection which means that a Volume 2 is more or less inevitable at some point.

For now, though, I hope you enjoy reading about the Society's blue plaques (and the one that isn't blue) and perhaps using this guide to explore the city's fascinating history on foot.

On behalf of the Society, I wish to express my thanks to Wakefield Council whose support by way of a Culture Grant as part of Our Year – Wakefield District 2024 has made this publication possible.

Kevin Trickett MBE
President
Wakefield Civic Society
October 2023

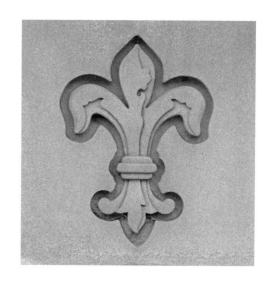

4.   The Blue Plaque Trails
4a. Northgate Trail

Wakefield City Centre (North)

Wrenthorpe

Stanley

1 Andrew Moynihan VC

WAKEFIELD CIVIC SOCIETY

ANDREW MOYNIHAN VC
(1830-1867)

AWARDED THE VICTORIA CROSS FOR GALLANTRY IN THE CRIMEAN WAR AT THE SIEGE OF SEBASTOPOL

BORN IN SAW YARD, WAKEFIELD AND BAPTISED IN THIS CHURCH ON 14 MARCH 1830

2013

📍 **St Austin's Church, Wentworth Terrace**

In 2011, the Society was contacted by local resident Mike Starford to enquire about the possibility of a blue plaque to Andrew Moynihan, the only Wakefield-born holder of a Victoria Cross medal. As a parishioner at St Austin's Roman Catholic Church in Wentworth Terrace, Mike was following up on research undetaken by fellow parishioner Agnes Hoban who had been prompted by a letter to *The Wakefield Express* in 1987 from a Mr Thomas Hird asking for information. Agnes discovered that the Moynihan family had also attended the same church in their time and that Andrew had been baptised there and would go on to attend the Church Sunday School. Andrew Moynihan was born on 1st January 1830 in Saw Yard, off Westgate.

As the family home was no longer standing, the church seemed a fitting place for the plaque and, fortunately, both the local priest, Fr Tim Swinglehurst, and the Leeds Diocese were in agreement. Moynihan would later move to live in Dukinfield in Lanarkshire and, at the age of 17, he enlisted in the 90th Regiment the Perthshire Volunteers. Following the outbreak of war in the Crimea in 1854, Moynihan was sent to fight. He was awarded the VC for gallantry shown on the field of battle on 8th September 1855 in the siege of Sebastopol. Moynihan died in Malta in 1867 having contracted brucellosis from drinking unpasteurised goat's milk. His Victoria Cross is displayed at the Cameronians Regimental Museum in Hamilton, Lanarkshire, Scotland.

This plaque was funded by the Cameronians (Scottish Rifles).

2 Wentworth House

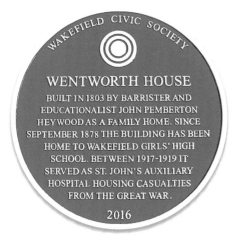

WAKEFIELD CIVIC SOCIETY

WENTWORTH HOUSE

BUILT IN 1803 BY BARRISTER AND EDUCATIONALIST JOHN PEMBERTON HEYWOOD AS A FAMILY HOME. SINCE SEPTEMBER 1878 THE BUILDING HAS BEEN HOME TO WAKEFIELD GIRLS' HIGH SCHOOL. BETWEEN 1917-1919 IT SERVED AS ST. JOHN'S AUXILIARY HOSPITAL HOUSING CASUALTIES FROM THE GREAT WAR.

2016

📍 **Wentworth Street**

In 2015, as part of their preparations to celebrate the 425th anniversary of the establishment of Queen Elizabeth Grammar School in Wakefield, the Wakefield Grammar School Foundation drew our attention to the fact that Wentworth House, now Wakefield Girls' High School, had been used as a St John's auxiliary hospital between 1917 and 1919 to treat casualties injured during the Great War.

The house was originally by in 1803 by barrister and educationalist John Pemberton Heywood (C.1755-1835) as a family home for himself, his wife Mary (née Drinkwater) and their children.

In 1878, the house was purchased by the Governors of the Grammar School from Elias Holt, a woollen manufacturer, as a base for a new 'ladies seminary' to educate up to 100 girls to university entrance standard[i].

This plaque was funded by the Wakefield Grammar School Foundation.

3 John Lee

WAKEFIELD CIVIC SOCIETY

RECORDS

JOHN LEE 1759 - 1836
THE LAWYER-ENTREPRENEUR WHO
DEVELOPED ST. JOHN'S SQUARE AND
INITIATED WHAT IS PROBABLY THE
FIRST PUBLIC RAILWAY, THE LAKE
LOCK RAIL ROAD, LIVED HERE
FROM 1802 UNTIL
HIS DEATH
1995

📍 **2 St John's Square**

This house in the corner of St John's Square was the home of John Lee (1759-1836) a Wakefield lawyer and property developer. In the 1790s and in partnership with local wool merchant Francis Maude (who was able to provide financial backing to begin with), Lee masterminded the building of the Square, originally known as St John's Place, together with its central church, and St John's North, originally called St John's Street. In effect, the St John's development was a 'new town' being somewhat removed from the dirt, noise and bustle of the then town centre.

The house is probably the best in the Square: the door facing onto the Square is actually a side door to the house; the main entrance to the front faces to the south and there is a substantial garden.

Lee's ambition and ingenuity lay behind many other local schemes including the Lake Lock railroad and the Wakefield and Aberford turnpike. He also built Balne Mill on Balne Lane for his son. Lee died in 1836 and is buried in the catacombs beneath Westgate Chapel[ii].

Today, Lee's house is home to the Junior School of Wakefield Girls' High School.

This plaque was funded with a grant from the National Lottery.

4 Constance Edith Heward

WAKEFIELD CIVIC SOCIETY

CONSTANCE EDITH
HEWARD
(1884-1968)

AUTHOR OF THE AMELIARANNE SERIES
OF CHILDREN'S BOOKS WHO RAN A
SMALL AND SUCCESSFUL PRIVATE
SCHOOL HERE IN THE 1930s
AND PRIOR TO THAT AT
BROMLEY MOUNT

2015

📍 **8 St John's Square**

Constance Heward was born in Derbyshire on 12th March 1884, the daughter of George Heward and Florence Nightingale Heward (née Whiteley). Her father died in 1913 while living in Worksop. Her mother died in 1926, while living in Wakefield.

The 1911 census shows that Heward was working as a nursery governess at 46 Derby Street, Bolton. At some point after this, she had moved to Wakefield where she was running a preparatory school at 5 Bromley Mount. By the 1930s, she had moved to 8 St John's Square from where she continued to run the school.

Meanwhile, she had also turned into quite a prolific author of children's books and short stories but is probably best known for writing eight of the 20 Ameliaranne Stories for girls. Heward eventually moved away from Wakefield and died in Ilkley in 1968.

The nomination for this plaque came from Kate Taylor who provided the above biographical details. It was unveiled by another member of Wakefield Civic Society, Constance Gilbey, who had been a pupil at the preparatory school when it was located at St John's Square.

This plaque was funded by the late Kate Taylor (see photo on page 5).

5 Wrenthorpe Potteries

WAKEFIELD CIVIC SOCIETY

POTTERIES WERE A FEATURE OF THIS AREA FROM MEDIEVAL TIMES, GIVING RISE TO THE OLD NAME OF 'POTOVENS'. OPPOSITE IS THE SITE OF ROBERT GLOVER'S POTTER'S COTTAGE, BUILT IN 1679, TOGETHER WITH SEVERAL 17th CENTURY POTTERY KILNS.

2005

📍 **The New Pot Oil Inn, 1 Wrenthorpe Lane**

There were small-scale potteries in the area now called Wrenthorpe from the late fifteenth century until the late eighteenth century. This was then a part of Wakefield's great 'out wood' (Outwood) and was known as Potovens on account of all the kilns or pot ovens to be found there.

Potters (also known as 'cuppers') built small bee-hive style kilns. A replica of one of these kilns stands today in front of the village hall.

Potteries were established here because of the ready availability of the necessary raw materials, clay, coal, water and wood and because of the demand for their products in nearby towns: pots produced here were sent to Pontefract, Leeds, Coventry and Leicester.

The industry here died out by 1785 as a result of increased competition from elsewhere, aided by better transport links[iii].

Some of the potteries were close to the location of The New Pot 'oil Inn and were excavated in 1983-4.

6 Queen Elizabeth Grammar School

WAKEFIELD CIVIC SOCIETY

QUEEN ELIZABETH GRAMMAR SCHOOL
DESIGNED BY RICHARD LANE AND ERECTED 1833-4, THIS BUILDING ORIGINALLY HOUSED THE WEST RIDING PROPRIETARY SCHOOL. QUEEN ELIZABETH GRAMMAR SCHOOL (QEGS) MOVED HERE IN 1854 FROM PREMISES IN BROOK STREET.

THIS PLAQUE COMMEMORATES THE 425th ANNIVERSARY OF THE FOUNDING OF QEGS IN 1591.

2016

📍 **Northgate**

Fourteen prominent citizens petitioned the monarch, Queen Elizabeth I, to grant a charter that would authorise the foundation of a free Grammar School in Wakefield. That charter was granted by the Queen on 15th November 1591 and work commenced on the building of a Grammar School around 1596, funds having by that time been raised for the construction to start. Wool merchant George Savile donated a plot of land in the Goodybower for the school, along with some stone from an adjoining quarry and some money. This original building, later extended but then reduced back to the original size, still stands in Brook Street.

Meanwhile, in Northgate, premises designed by Manchester architect Richard Lane were erected in 1833-34 for the West Riding Proprietary School. The Proprietary School ran into financial difficulties and the school premises were put up for sale – with the Grammar School acquiring the premises in 1854. The Northgate building has been the home of Queen Elizabeth Grammar School ever since.

The school celebrated its 425th anniversary in 2016 and asked the Society to erect a plaque to mark the occasion. The plaque is located on the gatepost to the school building in Northgate.

The plaque was funded by Wakefield Grammar School Foundation.

7   Sir Hubert Bennett and Bishopgarth

Westfield Road

Manchester architect Hubert Bennett (1909-2000) served as architect to West Riding County Council (WRCC) from 1945 to 1956. During that time, the Council's architects' department was based at Bishopgarth on Westfield Road. Bishopgarth, or the Bishop's Palace, was erected (1890-93) as a residence for the Bishops of Wakefield but was sold to the WRCC after Bishop Campbell Hone, appointed in 1938, decided it was unsuitable and suggested his own home in Sandal, later to become Bishop's Lodge, be used instead. WRCC then moved their architects' department into Bishopgarth.

During his tenure at the Council, Bennett designed new offices in the grounds of Bishopgarth and these were opened in 1950. In 1956, Bennett was appointed head of the architects' department at London County Council (later Greater London Council) where he oversaw the design of both the Hayward Gallery and the Queen Elizabeth Hall. Having been knighted in 1970, Bennett left local government and set up his own practice, working internationally on such buildings as the Palais des Festivals at Cannes and a palace for the Sultan of Oman in Muscat.

Bishopgarth was later used as a police training school but demolished in 2018 and the site developed for housing.

The current plaque was funded by Redrow.

8   Fanny Stott

Grove House, Westfield Road

When David and Eleanor Woollin moved into their house off College Grove Road, they discovered that a former occupant had been Fanny Stott, Wakefield's first female mayor.

Fanny Wordsworth Stott (1882-1961) was the daughter of corn miller Joseph Haslegrave, a councillor who would become Mayor of Wakefield in 1890, and his wife, (Fanny, née Wordsworth).

Fanny, one of 11 children, initially trained to be a nurse. In July 1914, she married Edwin Percival Stott, also a corn miller, at Sandal Church and, in 1917, their daughter, Ida Elizabeth (known as Betty) was born.

Fanny was elected as a Conservative Councillor in 1927 for the Eastmoor and St John's Ward. As well as being elevated to the Aldermanic Bench, she became a magistrate in 1939. In 1940/41, she served as the Mayor with her daughter Betty serving as Mayoress.

As a wartime mayor, Fanny raised money for many good causes, both locally and further afield. One of her fund-raising efforts was to help those affected by the Blitz in London.

This plaque was funded by David and Eleanor Woollin who additionally organised an unveiling event to raise money for the Mayor's Charity at the time.

9 Dame Barbara Hepworth

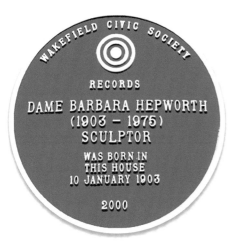

📍 15 Duke of York Street

One of Britain's most important sculptors, Barbara Hepworth DBE, was born here on 10 January 1903. She was the eldest child of Gertrude and Herbert Raikes Hepworth and was educated at Wakefield Girls' High School. In 1920, she started at the Leeds School of Art (where she met Henry Moore) before moving on (at the same time as Moore), to the Royal College of Art in London in 1921. After some years in Hampstead, she moved to St Ives where she died in an accidental fire at her studio in May 1975, aged 72.

Barbara married twice – first to sculptor John Skeaping (married in 1925, divorced in 1933) and then artist Ben Nicholson (married in 1938, divorced in 1951).

Barbara Hepworth was and remains an internationally recognised artist. Although mainly known for her modernist sculptures, she also produced drawings and lithographs. Barbara was made CBE in 1958 and DBE in 1965.

Today, Wakefield boasts an art gallery, The Hepworth Wakefield, opened in 2011, which, as well as displaying Wakefield's art collection and temporary exhibitions, also has galleries dedicated to the life and work of Barbara Hepworth.

This plaque was funded by a Millennium Lottery Grant.

10 Kenneth Leighton

📍 21 Denstone Street

This was the boyhood home of one of the most distinguished of British post-war composers. Kenneth Leighton (1929-1988) gained much of his early musical training as a chorister at Wakefield Cathedral whilst attending Queen Elizabeth Grammar School. He went on to Queen's College, Oxford, gaining degrees in both Classics and Music. Later, he taught at Leeds, Edinburgh and Oxford universities, becoming Reid Professor of Music in Edinburgh in 1970.

Leighton married twice – first to Lydia Angela Vignapiano whom he met while studying in Italy in 1951 and with whom he had two children, Angela and Robert. His second marriage was to Josephine Anne Prescott in 1981.

An outstanding keyboard performer and conductor as well as a prolific composer of many and varied works for voice, piano, chamber group and full orchestra, many of which are still available on CD.

This plaque was part-funded with a contribution from Wakefield Grammar School Foundation.

11 Nellie Spindler

WAKEFIELD CIVIC SOCIETY

STAFF NURSE NELLIE SPINDLER
(1891-1917)
LIVED AT 104 STANLEY ROAD AND WORKED AS A NURSE AT THE CITY FEVER HOSPITAL, LATER JOINING QUEEN ALEXANDRA'S IMPERIAL MILITARY NURSING SERVICE. KILLED BY SHELL-FIRE ON 21ST AUGUST 1917 AT BRANDHOEK, BELGIUM, SHE IS BURIED WITH FULL MILITARY HONOURS, THE ONLY WOMAN AMONGST OVER 10,000 MEN, AT THE COMMONWEALTH MILITARY CEMETERY AT LIJSSENTHOEK.

2017

⚲ 110 Stanley Road

Nellie Spindler was born in 1891 at the family home, 90 Carlton Street (Westgate End – and long since demolished). She was the first child of George and Elizabeth Spindler. The family moved to a terraced house at 74 Cleaver Place, later renumbered as 104 Stanley Road (the terrace has also been demolished and is now replaced with a modern block of flats and shops owned by WDH).

In 1910, at the age of 21, Spindler secured a position as an untrained nurse at the City of Wakefield Fever Hospital on Park Lodge Lane. She continued her training with service at Barnes Nursing Home in Scarborough and then at the Township Infirmary in Leeds.

Following the outbreak of war in 1915, Spindler enlisted with the Queen Alexandra's Imperial Military Nursing Service Reserve. She was posted to France in May 1917 and moved rapidly up the line to Brandhoek in Belgium where she served at No 44 Casualty Clearing Station. The hospital came under attack on the morning of 21st August 1917 and Spindler, who had just returned to her tent after night duty, was killed by the shrapnel from an exploding shell. She died in the arms of Nursing Sister Minnie Wood, also from Wakefield.

Spindler was buried with full military honours at the Commonwealth War Cemetery at Lijssenthoek, the only woman amongst over 10,000 men buried in the cemetery[iv].

This plaque was funded by WDH (Wakefield and District Housing Ltd).

12 Stanley Hall

WAKEFIELD CIVIC SOCIETY

RECORDS

STANLEY HALL, BUILT ABOUT 1802 FOR THE CLOTH-MERCHANT BENJAMIN HEYWOOD, WAS THE HOME OF WILLIAM SHAW (1804-1869), A SUCCESSFUL CONTRACTOR DURING THE GREAT AGE OF RAILWAY BUILDING IN THE 1840s.

2000

⚲ Aberford Road
(Opposite entrance to Bar Lane)

Originally built circa 1802 for cloth merchant Benjamin Heywood, Stanley Hall was the home from 1854 of William Shaw (1804-59). Shaw was a highly successful contractor during the great age of railway building in the 1830s. His career began building 'Gothic' churches and continued on the construction of the Macclesfield Canal before progressing to the Leeds and Selby Railway. He earned a considerable reputation in building railway tunnels including those at Chevet, Morley, Woodhead, and Woolley.

He also designed the almshouses in George Street provided by Caleb Crowther and the former Zion Chapel on the opposite side of George Street on the corner of Rodney Yard.

There is a vast monument to his memory in Wakefield cemetery.

This plaque was funded by a Millennium Lottery Grant.

⑬ Lake Lock Railroad

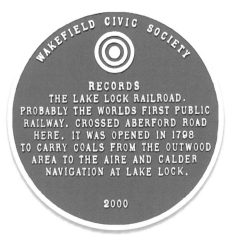

RECORDS
THE LAKE LOCK RAILROAD.
PROBABLY THE WORLDS FIRST PUBLIC
RAILWAY. CROSSED ABERFORD ROAD
HERE. IT WAS OPENED IN 1798
TO CARRY COALS FROM THE OUTWOOD
AREA TO THE AIRE AND CALDER
NAVIGATION AT LAKE LOCK.

2000

📍 **Stanley (Sited on the wall of the Sycamores, corner of Aberford Road and Lake Lock Road)**

The Lake Lock railroad was probably the world's first public railway – i.e. rather than being for the exclusive use of a particular company, it could be used by anybody for carrying goods upon payment of its tolls. It ran from Carr Gate for approximately three miles to the Aire and Calder Navigation at Lake Lock, carrying coals from the Outwood, and crossed the Aberford Road close to the point where the plaque is placed.

It was opened in 1798 and was used chiefly for the carrying of coal, stone, timber and burnt lime. It was later extended to Bottomboat and, in the opposite direction, to East Ardsley and Kirkhamgate.

The railroad, which would have used horse-drawn waggons eventually closed in 1836[v].

This plaque was funded by a Millennium Lottery Grant.

2017: The plaque for Nellie Spindler was unveiled at a Service of Remembrance at Wakefield Cathedral. This was followed by a short ceremony outside the shops in Stanley Road where the plaque was then erected.

4b. Wood Street Trail

Wakefield City Centre

Flanshaw

New Scarborough

14   Leatham, Tew and Co.

📍 **1–3 Wood Street**

The banking firm of Leatham, Tew and Co., originally established in Pontefract and Doncaster in 1801, opened their first branch in Wakefield in 1809, taking on the good will of customers from the failed Wakefield bank of Ingram and Kennet.

The banking operation on the corner of Wood Street, a site previously the location of the White Lion Inn, proved successful and enabled the bank to commission the building of new premises on the same site. The buildings that stand today, completed in 1881, were designed by the Leeds firm of J Neill and Son who were also responsible for Pontefract Infirmary.

The building is actually two buildings in one: the larger bank branch on the corner of Wood Street and a smaller building facing onto Wood Street which served as the bank manager's house. Leatham, Tew and Co. was absorbed by Barclays in 1906. The premises were vacated in 2012 when Barclays moved to Trinity Walk and the building lay empty until repurposed as the Qubana restaurant in 2017 when further changes were introduced to the interior and a new rear entrance created from George and Crown Yard.

This plaque was funded by Qubana.

15   Old Town Hall

📍 **Crown Court, Wood Street**

Tucked away in Crown Court, between Wood Street and King Street, stands the former Assembly Rooms which opened in 1798 (and now converted to residential use). Often referred to as the Music Hall in records from the time, the building also served from 1803 as a base of Wakefield's first newspaper, *The Wakefield Star* and *West Riding Advertiser*, and then for the Church Institute from 1845 to 1858.

Meanwhile, Wakefield became an incorporated borough in 1848 with elected councillors. The new Wakefield Corporation rented rooms in Barstow Square to begin with and held public meetings in buildings such as the Court House on Wood Street, but they really needed premises of their own.

However, the cost of building a new Town Hall from scratch proved daunting at a time when there were competing demands for the use of public funding. Following a fire at the former Assembly Rooms, the Council negotiated with the owner of the building to refurbish the premises with a council chamber and other facilities suited to their needs to become Wakefield's first Town Hall. This was agreed and the Council held their first meeting there in 1861. However, the building quickly proved to be too small and a new Town Hall was built in Wood Street.

This plaque was funded by Linfit Developments Ltd.

16 Mechanics' Institution

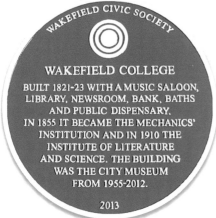

WAKEFIELD CIVIC SOCIETY

WAKEFIELD COLLEGE

BUILT 1821-23 WITH A MUSIC SALOON,
LIBRARY, NEWSROOM, BANK, BATHS
AND PUBLIC DISPENSARY.
IN 1855 IT BECAME THE MECHANICS'
INSTITUTION AND IN 1910 THE
INSTITUTE OF LITERATURE
AND SCIENCE. THE BUILDING
WAS THE CITY MUSEUM
FROM 1955-2012.

2013

📍 **Wood Street**

This building was originally built in 1820-1823 as Public Rooms with a music saloon on the upper floor. The Public Rooms housed a subscription library, a newsroom, a savings bank, and, in the basement, a company provided vapour, plunge and shower baths. In the 1820s and early 1830s, Wakefield's public dispensary occupied a part of the basement with residential accommodation for the apothecary and for two house servants. Wakefield's Mechanics' Institution, formed in 1841, leased the Music Saloon, later purchasing the building in 1855. The Music Saloon itself remained available for hire for public events. The building was renamed the Institute of Literature and Science in 1910.

By the 1930s, the Institute was failing. It was dissolved on 1st October 1935 and the trustees offered the building to the local authority. It was formally conveyed to Wakefield Corporation in December 1936. From 1955 until 2012, the building served as Wakefield Museum.

In 2012, the museum moved to Wakefield One and the building here was leased to Wakefield College who undertook major renovation work to convert the premises into a centre for performing arts, including a new 160-seat theatre, the Mechanics' Theatre, on the first floor.

Originally funded by Wakefield Council in 2007, the plaque was reworded in 2013 with the cost being met by Wakefield College.

17 Clayton Hospital

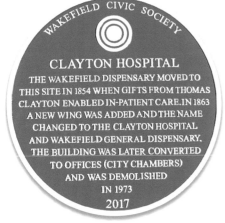

WAKEFIELD CIVIC SOCIETY

CLAYTON HOSPITAL

THE WAKEFIELD DISPENSARY MOVED TO
THIS SITE IN 1854 WHEN GIFTS FROM THOMAS
CLAYTON ENABLED IN-PATIENT CARE. IN 1863
A NEW WING WAS ADDED AND THE NAME
CHANGED TO THE CLAYTON HOSPITAL
AND WAKEFIELD GENERAL DISPENSARY.
THE BUILDING WAS LATER CONVERTED
TO OFFICES (CITY CHAMBERS)
AND WAS DEMOLISHED
IN 1973

2017

📍 **Between Wood Street and Northgate (plaque sited on Cross Street)**

The first public dispensary in Wakefield dates from 1787. At that time, it was based in a house at the Kirkgate end of Northgate, adjacent to the parish church (now the Cathedral). The dispensary moved to the basement of the Public Rooms in Wood Street in the 1820s when the original house was demolished. However, the basement proved so unhealthy that the apothecary died and the dispensary was re-located to a house in Barstow Square.

In 1854, the dispensary moved again, this time to a house between Northgate and Wood Street, accessed via Dispensary Yard in Northgate.

A gift from Wakefield businessman Thomas Clayton enabled the dispensary to be extended by the building of wards and later a new wing. The name of the dispensary was changed to Clayton Hospital and Dispensary. A bequest in the will of Thomas Clayton, who died in 1868, enabled the building of a completely new hospital between Northgate and Wentworth Street. The building in Wood Street was extended upwards and converted to offices, becoming the offices of the Inland Revenue until it was finally demolished in 1973.

This plaque was funded by Woodhead Investments.

18 Tammy Hall

WAKEFIELD CIVIC SOCIETY

RECORDS
THIS BUILDING IS THE SURVIVING
PART OF THE TAMMY (CLOTH) HALL.
OPENED IN 1777.
IN 1878 IT BECAME THE BOROUGH'S
FIRE AND POLICE STATION,
AS THE CARVINGS SHOW.

2000

📍 **Cliff Parade**

In the eighteenth century, Wakefield was a major centre for the wool trade. Raw wool as well as finished cloth was sold here. In 1777, a cloth hall was built here for the sale of tammies and camlets, types of worsted cloths. The building was 230 feet long by 33 feet wide and had 200 stalls over two floors. On the roof was a bell turret and it was the ringing of the bell on Friday mornings at 11am that signalled the start of trading.

Unfortunately, the Wakefield trade was relatively short-lived as merchants took their business to nearby towns such as Bradford and Halifax. The building was later used as a warehouse and then a mill for the production of worsted goods until 1863.

In 1865, the building was used for the Wakefield Industrial and Fine Art Exhibition which ran from 30th August to 19th October that year. To accommodate the exhibition, the building was given a temporary glass and timber extension facing onto Wood Street (where the Town Hall stands today). The building was further modified in the 1870s when part of its length was demolished (to create space for the Town Hall) and the width doubled along the King Street elevation to create a new police and fire station, opening in 1878. The building later became Wakefield Magistrates Courts (until 2016) but is today converted into apartments.

This plaque was funded by a Millennium Lottery grant but was refurbished in 2023 at the Society's expense.

19 County Hall

WAKEFIELD CIVIC SOCIETY

COUNTY HALL

OPENED ON 22ND FEB. 1898 AND BUILT ON THE
SITE OF THE FORMER RISHWORTH HOUSE TO A
DESIGN BY ARCHITECT JAMES S GIBSON, THIS
WAS THE SEAT OF THE WEST RIDING COUNTY
COUNCIL UNTIL 1974, THEN WEST YORKSHIRE
COUNTY COUNCIL UNTIL ITS ABOLITION
IN 1986. ACQUIRED BY THE CITY OF
WAKEFIELD METROPOLITAN
DISTRICT COUNCIL IN 1987.

2018

📍 **Bond Street**

The Local Government Act of 1888 established an administrative boundary centred on the West Riding of Yorkshire. This in turn led to the creation of the West Riding County Council (WRCC), set up to administer the new county. The new County Council came into being in 1889 and held its first meeting at the Town Hall in February of that year. The County Council had acquired Rishworth House (a house built for the Rishworth family in 1812) and this was demolished to create a space for the new County Hall. Work started on the building you see today in 1894 with the building being opened in 1898.

An architectural competition was held to select the design and this was won by Scottish-born, but London-based, architect James Glen Sivewright Gibson (1861-1951) who, at one time, worked for Thomas Colcutt, architect of Wakefield's Town Hall. County Hall was extended in matching style between 1912 and 1915.

WRCC was abolished in 1974 but replaced by the West Yorkshire County Council. After this too was closed down (in 1986), the building was acquired in 1987 by Wakefield Council who use the council chamber on the first floor for meetings of the elected members.

The plaque was funded by Wakefield Council.

20 Sir Alec Clegg

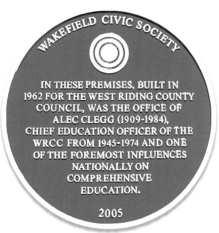

8 Bond Street

Alexander Bradshaw Clegg (1909-1986 – not 1984 as on the plaque[vi]) was born in Long Eaton Derbyshire, the son of a schoolmaster, and attended Long Eaton Grammar School. He later attended Bootham School in York before securing a place at Cambridge University where he achieved a first in Modern Languages. He then took the London teaching diploma and worked as a teacher from 1932–36. After periods working for the education departments of Birmingham, Cheshire, and Worcestershire education authorities, he was appointed to the post of Deputy Education Officer of the West Riding in 1945 at the age of 34.

Nine months later, he was promoted to Chief Education Officer of the West Riding County Council, serving in the role from 1945-1974.

He was a major advocate for comprehensive schools and stressed the central role of art, music, drama and physical education in developing the rounded human being. He saw Bretton Hall established as a place for training teachers in Art, Music and Drama, and Lady Mabel College, Wentworth Woodhouse, for the training of PE teachers. His positions included being chairman of the Yorkshire Television advisory committee. He was knighted in 1965.

21 The West Riding Registry of Deeds

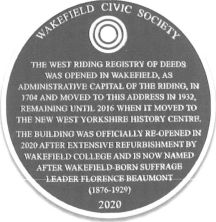

Corner of Newstead Road and Margaret Street

The West Riding magistrates were one of the first authorities in the country to provide for the registration of deeds and especially those relating to the transfer of property. The Registry of Deeds opened in 1704. The vast bound volumes, assembled by date, were transferred to these purpose-built premises in Newstead Road in 1932. The building also housed the Wakefield and West Riding collections of the West Yorkshire Archive Service. The Society erected a blue plaque in 1995, funded by a National Lottery grant.

In 2016, the Registry of Deeds and the other collections were transferred to a new building in Lower Kirkgate, the West Yorkshire History Centre and the Newstead Road building was taken on by Wakefield College who embarked on an extensive programme of refurbishment to convert the building into teaching accommodation, including Gaskell's Restaurant which had previously been housed in a College building off Margaret Street.

The newly refurbished building was re-opened in 2020 and is now known as the Beaumont Building, named after Wakefield-born suffrage leader Florence Beaumont. Our new blue plaque was unveiled as part of the opening ceremonies.

This new plaque was funded by Wakefield College.

22 Sir John Wolfenden

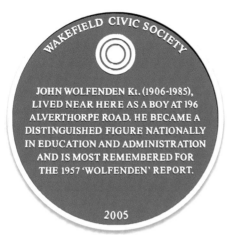

📍 **Balne Lane Community Centre, junction of Balne Lane and Alverthorpe Road.**

196 Alverthorpe Road was the boyhood home of John Wolfenden (1906-1985). Born in Swindon, Wiltshire, the son of Yorkshire parents, he came to Wakefield as a boy in 1912 when his father joined the staff of the West Riding Education Authority. He attended Queen Elizabeth Grammar School and then Queen's College, Oxford, taking a First in Greats (Classics).

Wolfenden had a distinguished career in education taking headships at Uppingham and Shrewsbury, then vice-chancellor of Reading University in 1950.

He became chairman of the University Grants Committee and finally the director and principal librarian of the British Museum. He was granted a peerage in 1974.

Today, he is perhaps best known for his 1957 report *The Report of the Departmental Committee on Homosexual Offences and Prostitution* (often referred to as just 'The Wolfenden Report'), recommending reforms to the laws on prostitution and homosexuality. These recommendations were eventually taken up by Parliament and given legal effect in the Sexual Offences Act of 1967[vii].

This plaque was part-funded with a contribution from Wakefield Grammar School Foundation.

23 Sirdar

📍 **Bective Mills, Flanshaw Lane, Alverthorpe**

Brothers Tom and Henry Harrap established a yarn manufacturing business in Ossett in 1880 but later moved to the current site at Flanshaw in 1890. The company adopted the name Sirdar in 1934 and became a world leader in the production of knitting wool and knitting patterns. Customers could buy a pattern and the wool needed to make up the garment at one go.

The company continued in family ownership and, from 1960, was led by Jean Tyrell (née Harrap, daughter of Fred who died that year). The company was taken over in 2007 (and since been taken over again).

At the unveiling of the plaque, guests were shown around the premises where we learned that, although wool was no longer actually spun at the mill, it was still packed and dispatched from there – and customers can still order the wool to make up specific garments using the yarn patterns supplied by the company. Meanwhile, the company also produces specialised fabrics for use in such things as anti-stab vests, butcher's gloves and in the interiors of high-performance cars.

This plaque was funded by Sirdar Spinning Ltd.

24 Percy Metcalfe

PERCY METCALFE
CVO RDI
(1895-1970)
SCULPTOR AND DESIGNER
WAS BORN AND RAISED HERE. STUDIED AT THE
LEEDS SCHOOL OF ART FROM 1910 TO 1914
AND AFTER AT THE ROYAL COLLEGE OF ART.

HIS DESIGNS WERE USED IN COINS AND MEDALS,
INCLUDING THE GEORGE CROSS MEDAL,
AND IN POTTERY, CAR MASCOTS AND
COMMEMORATIVE MONUMENTS.

2021

📍 **10 Longfield Terrace, Alverthorpe**

One of the joys of the Society's blue plaque scheme is the way it brings to light the stories of local people whose histories have been overlooked, if not forgotten, in their home city. One such individual is Percy Metcalfe, born (on 14th January 1895) and raised at Longfield Terrace in Alverthorpe, but practically unknown today in Wakefield.

Metcalfe began his arts education when he commenced a period of study at the Leeds School of Art from 1910 to 1914. He won a Royal Exhibition scholarship to the Royal College of Art where he studied from 1914 to 1915 when, with the outbreak of war, he joined the Royal Field Artillery. He was badly wounded while serving in France and did not return to the College in London until 1915.

The war injury to his leg was to cause long-lasting health problems which meant that Metcalfe had to give up working on large sculpture. However, he did continue to design coins, commemorative medals, war memorials and monuments, car mascots, pottery and even shop interiors. His coin designs were chosen for the first currency of the Irish Free State in 1926 by a committee chaired by the poet W.B. Yeats. In 1940, his design was also chosen for the George Cross Medal.

Metcalfe was awarded the CVO (Commander of the Royal Victorian Order) in 1937 and, in 1938, he was appointed a Royal Designer for Industry (RDI). He died in London, where he lived, in 1970[viii].

This plaque was funded by Wakefield Civic Society member Geoff Wood.

The Westgate Heritage Action Zone

In 2019, the Society was invited by Wakefield Council to participate in a new project.

A bid for government funding was being submitted to Historic England to establish a High Street Heritage Action Zone in Upper Westgate, mapping onto the existing Conservation Area. The bid was successful and a grant of nearly £2M was awarded, which was then match-funded by the Council to provide a project budget of almost £4M. The project aimed to improve the condition of the public realm and certain key buildings in the Upper Westgate area. Grants of up to 90% of the cost of the work were made available to property owners.

One important aspect of the project was community engagement. As part of that engagement, the Society, along with Wakefield Historical Society, were awarded funding to undertake research into the history of the area and to publish the findings by way of books, pamphlets and on-line articles.

Additionally, the Civic Society was asked to lead guided walks and given additional funding to put up new plaques and refurbish older plaques that were in need of attention.

The Society's book, *Westgate Wakefield*, published in 2022 tells the history of the buildings in Wakefield and is available separately.

4c. Westgate Trail

Wakefield City Centre

BURTON ST
CLIFF PDE
CROSS ST
WOOD ST
GEORGE AND CROWN YD
KING ST
WOOLPACK'S YD
MULBERRY WAY
DRURY LN
CARTER ST
CHEAPSIDE
MARYGATE
WESTGATE
SMYTH ST
WHITE HORSE YD
MARKET ST
QUEEN ST

28
32 31
30
29 37
33
38 39
27
26 25
41
40
36

34 0.1 mi
35 1.2 mi

N

Lower Westgate

Westgate
BACK LN
WESTGATE
City Centre
WESTGATE END
QUEBEC ST
INGS RD
34

N

Lupset

DEWSBURY RD
HASELDEN RD
GEORGE A GREEN RD
WATERTON RD
City Centre
35

N

25 The Woolpacks

Woolpacks Yard, Westgate

The Woolpacks Inn (also referred to as the Woolpack and the Wool-Pack, etc) served as a coaching inn. Set back up a yard leading off Westgate, the Inn would have had ancillary buildings including stabling for the horses.

The inn and associated plot was redeveloped in 1774 by wool merchant Thomas Crowther. He built a new house for himself, facing onto Westgate, just to the right of what is today Woolpacks Yard, and a neighbouring house next door, just to the left of Barstow Square. These houses became shops in the late 19th century and a bank in the 20th. After the bank moved out, the buildings were turned into a nightclub.

Today, the buildings have been restored to their 1920s appearance as part of the Heritage Action Zone project, albeit as a bar rather than a bank.

Meanwhile, up Woolpacks Yard, stands the former Inn, later operated as a bar but now, at the time of writing, being converted into residential use.

This plaque was funded by a grant from the Heritage Action Zone project.

26 George Gissing

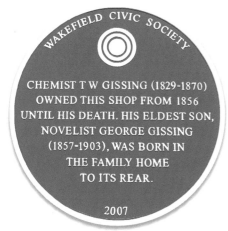

NatWest Bank, 60 Westgate

This shop, part of premises built c1850, was a chemist's from then until the 1970s. Pharmaceutical chemist Thomas Waller Gissing (1829-1870) owned it from 1856 until his death. His eldest son, novelist George Gissing, was born in 1857 in the family home in Thompson's Yard behind the shop where a museum, run by the Gissing Trust, now celebrates the author's work and life.

George Gissing wrote 23 novels, including *New Grub Street*, two studies of Dickens, a travel book and numerous short stories.

Although after his father's death Gissing never lived permanently in Wakefield, his recollections of his hometown, its landscape and some of its citizens colour some of his novels and short stories. *A Life's Morning* in particular has Wakefield as its setting and reflects a period spent at his mother's home, then in Stoneleigh Terrace, Doncaster Road.

After periods living in the USA and London, George Gissing died in France in 1903.

This plaque was part funded by Wakefield Council.

27 Wool Market

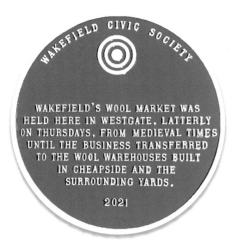

HSBC, 66 Westgate

Westgate was long the scene of Wakefield's thriving corn, wool and livestock markets with the actual markets being held in the street.

Wool-staplers bought raw wool from farmers, sorted and graded it into bales which were stored in warehouses and sold on to small manufacturers, many who were part of a 'cottage industry' of spinners, working from home to begin with but later in mills, turning the raw wool into cloth. Wool-staplers would then buy the cloth and dye and finish it to sell or make clothes that could be sold.

As with the corn and malt markets, wool bales were laid out at the top of Westgate but, as the market grew, warehouses were built in the yards off Westgate, particularly along Cheapside to where the wool market moved at the beginning of the 19th century[ix].

See also plaque No. 28 at 19 Cheapside.

This plaque was originally funded by a Millennium Lottery grant in 2000 but was refurbished in 2021 with the cost of refurbishment being met by HSBC.

28 19 Cheapside

19 Cheapside

As explained in the entry for plaque 27, the original site of the wool market in the medieval period was the top of Westgate. Wakefield was a significant market town and market stalls stood in the main streets which were, in effect, zoned with different markets held in different parts of the medieval town centre.

Cheapside was opened up for development in the early 19th century. The site of today's street had previously been a narrow yard behind a house on Westgate which was demolished. By 1802, warehouses such as this one at 19 Cheapside, had appeared. The warehouses were used to store the bales of wool and the wool trade moved into the warehouses[x].

Cheapside today still shows its early origins with many of the buildings bearing witness to their use as warehouses. Look for oversized central windows, which would have originally been doors that opened to allow goods to be hoisted up and into the different floors from horse-drawn carts outside. Stand at the opposite side of the street and look up at the top central window of No. 19, and you will see that the hoist is still there.

This plaque was funded by a grant from the Heritage Action Zone project.

29 The Picture House

📍 **Westgate**

This is Wakefield's first purpose-built cinema (although other cinemas had been opened in other buildings adapted for the purpose). Commissioned by former theatre manager Sydney Tolfree, the building had seats for 1,480 patrons. The cinema was also used to stage plays (a retaliation of sorts to the Theatre Royal's decision to screen films!) and the name was changed to the Playhouse Cinema. However, the original name of Picture House remained on the front of the building (which is actually finished in terracotta tiles).

The cinema was purchased by the Rank Organisation in the mid-1970s and it was later converted into a nightclub – Casanova's. At some point in the conversion, the building lost its canopy above the central door, now a window.

The building's exterior was refurbished as part of the Heritage Action Zone project and the lettering and other details picked out in green. Above where the central entrance used to be, you can still see the two hooks from which was suspended the entrance canopy.

This plaque was funded by a grant from the Heritage Action Zone project.

30 Theatre Royal Wakefield

📍 **Drury Lane**

The first theatre on this site was built in 1776 by James Banks, a wool merchant who lived in the house in Drury Lane that is today the York House Hotel. The theatre could accommodate around 1,000 audience members – but seated on rudimentary benches and cane chairs, or standing. Unlike today, where the theatre operates year-round, the earlier theatre would have opened only in September to coincide with the horse-racing season at the Outwood racecourse.

The theatre was condemned by the West Riding County Council in 1892 because it failed the safety standards of the day and a new building, designed by well-known theatre architect Frank Matcham (1854-1920), built on the site. (Matcham also design the Tower Ballroom in Blackpool, the London Coliseum and the London Palladium among many others.) The new theatre opened in 1894. It was used as a cinema from 1954 to 1966, re-opening as a bingo hall in the 1970s. A project to restore the building led to its re-opening as a theatre in 1986. A modern extension opened alongside in 2018.

This plaque was funded by Theatre Royal Wakefield.

31 John Goodchild Collection

Rear of The Art House, Mulberry Way

To anyone with an interest in local history, John Goodchild (1935-2017) hardly needs an introduction. Over his lifetime, he built up a huge collection of artefacts, historic documents, books and maps which were housed in rooms at the rear of the former Drury Lane Library.

On his death, Goodchild donated his collection to Wakefield Council who have passed it into the care of the West Yorkshire Archive Service and it is now located in the West Yorkshire History Centre in Lower Kirkgate.

The collection was organised to suit the way that Goodchild worked and much of it stored in boxes – a system almost impenetrable to others!

On accepting the collection, the Council and Archive Service recognised that it would be necessary to arrange for a professional archivist to undertake a review of the collection and begin indexing the contents. The blue plaque was unveiled in 2019 to mark not only the formal handing over of the collection but also the beginning of the project to index it in line with standard methodologies.

This plaque was funded by Alan Hughes, who was John's partner, Peter Brears and Richard Knowles.

32 The Orangery and Lodge

Corner of Back Lane and Mulberry Way

The Orangery was a garden building for Pemberton House, the Georgian house at 122 Westgate (see plaque No. 33). After the death of both Pemberton Milnes in 1795 and his wife, Jane, in 1812, the house was inherited by their daughter, Bridget, the Dowager Viscountess Galway.

Bridget is thought to have built the Orangery at some point after her father's death, possibly around 1800 and before she married the Viscount in 1803.

Early maps suggest that the building seen today has been extended more than once.

The buildings and land were leased from 1839 and run as zoological and botanical gardens (until, in 1844, a bear escaped and attacked the parkkeeper's sister-in-law, fatally wounding her). The Orangery was purchased by Wakefield's first MP, Daniel Gaskell, of Lupset Hall in 1849 and he gifted the building and grounds to the trustees of the Unitarian Chapel to use as a school.

The Lodge appears to date from around 1850 and is thought to be a replacement for an earlier building, probably demolished to make way for the railway.

This plaque was funded by a grant from the Heritage Action Zone project.

33 Pemberton Milnes House

PEMBERTON HOUSE WAS BUILT IN 1754 FOR PEMBERTON MILNES 1729 – 1795, CLOTH MERCHANT, ACTIVE MAGISTRATE AND LEADER OF THE DISSENTING WHIG POLITICAL INTEREST IN THE WEST RIDING

2022

📍 122 Westgate

This was the home of Pemberton Milnes (1729-1795), a member of a family of prosperous cloth merchants who built Back Lane Mill (demolished when the railway station was built). With his brother John, Milnes was an investor in both the Halifax Piece Hall and the Leeds Cloth Hall[xi]. Milnes was a leading Whig of his day, a West Riding magistrate and, from 1776 a deputy lieutenant of the county.

In the 1840s and 50s the house was the home of Henry Clarkson, surveyor and author of *Memories of Merry Wakefield*.

The house was compulsorily purchased by the West Riding and Grimsby Railway and was used as a base for *The Wakefield and West Riding Herald*, a local newspaper, from circa 1872 to 1910.

Later, from 1920 to 1946 approximately, it was used as the Labour Exchange and then as offices of the London, Midland and Scottish Railway (British Rail 1946-c1973)[xii].

More recently, it has been used as charity offices but was purchased by Wakefield Council to be part of a redevelopment project for the former Westgate Station site.

This plaque was originally funded in 1995 by a National Lottery grant but was refurbished in 2022 with the cost of refurbishment being met by the Heritage Action Zone project.

34 House of Correction

RECORDS

THE WEST RIDING HOUSE OF CORRECTION (PRISON) OPENED ON THIS SITE IN 1595. IT CAME UNDER GOVERNMENT MANAGEMENT IN 1878.

2000

📍 Corner of Back Lane and Westgate

The West Riding Magistrates opened a prison here in the 1595. It was the result of a bequest by barrister George Savile who died in December 1594. His will reads, 'I give twenty pounds for and towards the building of a House of Correction within seven miles of Wakefield for the setting of the poor on work....' The prison was rebuilt in 1770, albeit a little to the north, farther back from Westgate. It passed from the magistrates into central government control under the 1877 Prisons Act.

The prison was rebuilt yet again in 1884 with the entrance on Love Lane, to the side of the existing building.

Until 1773, inmates had to pay their gaolers fees for their accommodation[xiii].

This plaque was funded by a Millennium Lottery grant.

35 David Storey

WAKEFIELD CIVIC SOCIETY

THE BOYHOOD HOME OF
DAVID STOREY
(1933-2017),
RUGBY FOOTBALLER,
NOVELIST AND PLAYWRIGHT,
MUCH OF WHOSE WORK
REFLECTS HIS YEARS
IN WAKEFIELD

2019

📍 91 Manor Haigh Road

Novelist and playwright David Storey (1933-2017) lived in this former council house throughout his boyhood. He attended Queen Elizabeth Grammar School and then the Slade School of Fine Art in London. To support himself, he played rugby for Leeds RUFC.

Storey won the Booker Prize in 1976 for his novel *Saville* although he is probably better known today for his 1960 novel, *This Sporting Life* for which he won the MacMillan Fiction Award. *This Sporting Life* was made into a film shortly afterwards and Storey wrote the screenplay.

Storey continued to write novels and both his novels and plays draw on his formative years in Wakefield and his knowledge of the local landscape. His last novel was *Thin-Ice Skater* (2004) although he also published an autobiography, *A Stinging Delight*, in 2021.

Storey lived in London where he died in 2017 survived by his four children, his wife Barbara (née Rudd) having predeceased him in 2015. Unusually, the blue plaque was first erected in 2000, during Storey's lifetime.

This plaque was originally funded by a Millennium Lottery grant but was refurbished in 2019, when Storey's year of death was added. The cost of the refurbishment was met by WDH (Wakefield and District Housing Ltd).

36 Bank House

WAKEFIELD CIVIC SOCIETY

BANK HOUSE
BUILT C.1790 AS A LUXURIOUS MANSION HOUSE FOR THE
INGRAM FAMILY OF WAKEFIELD BANKING FIRM INGRAM
AND KENNET. THE PROPERTY WAS SOLD FOLLOWING
THE BANK'S COLLAPSE IN 1812. FROM 1825 TO 1829 IT
WAS OWNED BY THE BANKING FIRM OF WENTWORTH,
CHALONER AND RISHWORTH. AFTER THAT BANK
ALSO COLLAPSED, THE PROPERTY WAS ACQUIRED
BY THE WAKEFIELD BANKING COMPANY, LATER
THE WAKEFIELD AND BARNSLEY UNION
BANK, ESTABLISHED IN 1832. IT WAS
LATER SUB-DIVIDED AND USED AS
OFFICES FOR MANY YEARS.

2022

📍 67 Westgate

This house and its neighbour at No. 65 Westgate (see entry 37 below) have a shared pedigree. No. 67 was built as the mansion house for Frances Ingram (1739-1815). Ingram was born in Oulton but moved to Liverpool where he was partner in the bank of Staniforth, Ingram, Bold and Daltera. Ingram built his fortune from the slave trade and appears to have used the profits to finance his banking operations. Ingram inherited the family fortune, including land and buildings in Westgate where his mother, Sarah, had owned the Star Inn in Star Yard (now Bank Street). He returned to Wakefield in 1785 where he opened the bank of Ingram and Kennet.

The bank foundered in 1812 and assets, including Ingram's mansion, were sold to pay creditors. (Ingram left England and died in Rome in 1815). The house was then acquired by Thomas Rishworth, who had been the first clerk of Ingram and Kennet, but who had joined the banking firm of Wentworth, Chaloner and Rishworth and the house appears to have been used as a bank. That bank also failed and the property was acquired by the Wakefield Banking Company, later the Wakefield and Barnsley Union Bank (see entry No. 38).

The original plaque on this property was erected in 1995 and was funded by a National Lottery grant. The new plaque was funded by a grant from the Heritage Action Zone project.

37 Ingram and Kennet

WAKEFIELD CIVIC SOCIETY

WAKEFIELD'S FIRST PURPOSE-BUILT BANK, BUILT FOR THE BANKING FIRM OF INGRAM AND KENNET (ESTABLISHED IN 1785). IN 1840 THE WAKEFIELD AND BARNSLEY UNION BANK TOOK OVER THE PROPERTY WITH THEIR SECOND BANK MANAGER, WILLIAM HEY DYKES, LIVING IN THE PREMISES BEHIND FROM 1841. AMONG DYKES' CHILDREN WERE HYMN COMPOSERS JOHN BACCHUS DYKES AND ELIZA SIBBALD DYKES. ELIZA WAS ALSO A POET AND PAINTER WHOSE WORK WAS DISPLAYED IN THE CORN EXCHANGE IN 1870 ALONGSIDE THAT OF ARTIST LOUISA FENNELL.

2022

📍 65 Westgate

This building was Wakefield's first purpose-built bank, designed for the banking firm of Ingram and Kennet (see entry No. 36) and was erected in the 1790s. Kennet lived in residential accommodation behind the bank down White Horse Yard. Following the failure of that bank in 1812, it was later taken over by the Wakefield and Barnsley Union Bank (established in 1832 - see plaque 38 below). The second manager of the new bank was William Hey Dykes. He and his family lived in accommodation behind the bank from 1841 onwards. Among the Dykes children were John Bacchus Dykes who became one of the most prolific composers of hymn tunes, many of which are still very well known today, and Eliza Sibald Dykes (Alderson on marriage), also a composer of hymns as well as being a poet and painter. Some of her paintings were displayed at an exhibition held in the Corn Exchange in 1870 alongside work of another Wakefield artist, Louisa Fennell. Another son, Frederick, would take over responsibility for running the bank, becoming the bank manager in 1857 when William retired[xiv].

After the building ceased to be used for banking purposes, it was converted into a furniture shop. Most recently, it has been used as a bar and nightclub.

This plaque was funded by a grant from the Heritage Action Zone project.

38 The Wakefield and Barnsley Union Bank

WAKEFIELD CIVIC SOCIETY

DESIGNED BY H.F. LOCKWOOD, THESE PREMISES WERE BUILT IN 1877-8 FOR THE WAKEFIELD AND BARNSLEY UNION BANK, WHICH WAS FOUNDED IN 1832 AND REMAINED INDEPENDENT UNTIL 1906

2019

📍 57 Westgate

This magnificent building was designed by Henry Francis Lockwood in 1877-8 for the Wakefield and Barnsley Union Bank. (Lockwood established a partnership with William Mawson in 1849 and moved to Bradford in 1850 from where the two designed a number of prominent buildings in the town.)

The Wakefield and Barnsley Union Bank, by then managed by Frederick Dykes (see entry No. 37), moved here from its more modest premises lower down Westgate. In 1906, it was taken over by the Birmingham, District & Counties Banking Co. Ltd. which, as the United Counties Bank Ltd., was in turn acquired by Barclays Bank in 1916.

The building then became home to the ill-fated Wakefield Building Society where, in the 1970s, a shock discovery was made that the present and previous general managers of the Building Society had, over many years, embezzled a fortune. The Building Society merged with the Halifax Building Society who sold the premises which then became a bar and nightclub.

In 2019, the bar, now in new ownership, underwent a major renovation, re-opening as Union Bank with meeting rooms and a sales centre on the upper floors.

This plaque was originally funded by a Millennium Lottery grant but was refurbished in 2019 with the cost being met by Craft Union Pubs.

39 The Great Bull Hotel

51–55 Westgate

An inn has stood on this site since at least 1635. The current building dates from the 1770s. As one of Wakefield's most important inns, it is perhaps not surprising to learn that the yard at the rear had stabling for nearly 100 horses. The yard was accessed through an archway in the centre of the front façade.

By the start of the 20th century, the hotel trade had started to decline and the building was acquired by the Prudential Assurance Company and the building became known as Prudential Buildings. The company made some significant changes to the premises which it shared with other businesses including the Great Bull Restaurant.

The Prudential moved out and, by 1951, Martins Bank had moved in, occupying No. 55 Westgate, the part of the building to the right when viewed from the front. When Martins merged with Barclays, the building was occupied by a firm of solicitors but, at the beginning of the 21st century, its use had reverted to being a place for leisure with a nightclub and bars opening. Today, the ground floor continues to operate as bars but the upper floors are now home to Westgate Studios.

This plaque was funded by a grant from the Heritage Action Zone project.

40 Corn Exchange

Corner of Market Street and Westgate

Wakefield's corn market, originally held in the street at the top of Westgate where bags of corn and barley were laid out for sale, was the largest in the north of England. As the market prospered, a Corn Exchange was built at the top of Westgate (between today's Silver Street and Marygate). It opened in 1820 but soon proved too small and a larger building was built opposite.

The plaque here marks the site of this second Corn Exchange, built in the great classical style to a design by Scottish-born, but Doncaster-based, architect William Lambie Moffat (who adopted the spelling of his surname as Moffatt).

The Assembly Rooms on the first floor of the handsome building were in frequent use in the Victorian period for concerts, bazaars and all manner of public meetings. In 1858, Charles Dickens read *A Christmas Carol* there[xv]. In the early twentieth century the Exchange floor became a roller-skating rink and the Assembly Rooms were converted in 1910 into the Grand Electric Cinema, Wakefield's first cinema. Business dropped off and, following a fire in 1957, the building was demolished in 1962.

The plaque was originally funded by a Millennium Lottery grant but was refurbished in 2022 with the cost being met by a grant from the Heritage Action Zone project.

41 Manor Bakehouse

WAKEFIELD CIVIC SOCIETY

NEAR THIS SITE STOOD THE
PUBLIC BAKEHOUSE OF THE
LORDS OF THE MANOR OF WAKEFIELD.
IT WAS DEMOLISHED IN 1861 TO MAKE
WAY FOR THE CHURCH INSTITUTE,
LATER YOUTH HOUSE.

2022

📍 **Marygate**

A public bakehouse was provided on this site from medieval times, by the lord of the manor, for the use of Wakefield people who were obliged to use its facilities. This spared them lighting substantial fires in their own homes for baking bread, pies, etc. and was an important facility in a town where most of the buildings were made of wood and hence highly combustible. Bread from the bakehouse would be sold in the bread booths on today's Bread Street.

The bakehouse was demolished in 1861 and new premises for the Church Institute erected on the site.

This too was demolished in 1964, along with other old buildings adjacent, to create space for new shops with offices above (which are being converted to residential at the time of writing).

The plaque was originally funded by a Millennium Lottery grant but was refurbished in 2022 with the cost being met by a grant from the Heritage Action Zone project.

4d. Kirkgate Trail

Wakefield City Centre (South)

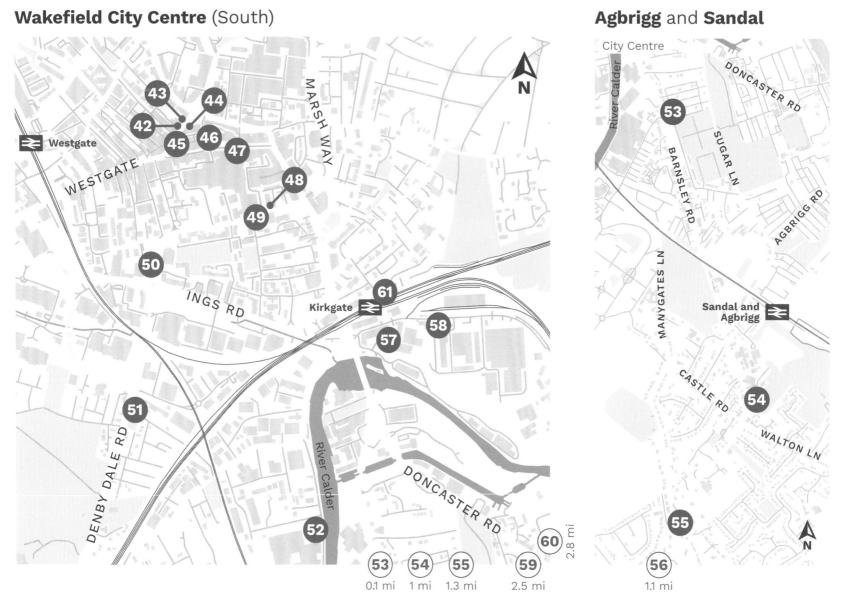

Westgate

43 44 42 45 46 47 48 49

MARSH WAY

WESTGATE

50

INGS RD

Kirkgate 61

58

57

DENBY DALE RD

51

River Calder

52

DONCASTER RD

60 2.8 mi

53 0.1 mi 54 1 mi 55 1.3 mi 59 2.5 mi

Agbrigg and Sandal

City Centre

River Calder

DONCASTER RD

53

SUGAR LN

BARNSLEY RD

AGBRIGG RD

MANYGATES LN

Sandal and Agbrigg

CASTLE RD

54

WALTON LN

55

56 1.1 mi

42 Dr John Radcliffe

◉ Radcliffe Place, off the Bull Ring

Dr John Radcliffe (1650-1714) is reputed to have lived near here as a boy. His father George was the governor of the Wakefield House of Correction and established a printworks in the yard.

Radcliffe was a pupil at Queen Elizabeth Grammar School before going on to University College, Oxford. He then became a fellow of Lincoln College there. He began studying medicine, obtaining a degree in 1675. He moved to London in 1684, building up a substantial practice and in 1686 became physician to Princess Anne of Denmark.

Later he was appointed physician to William and Mary. A number of key buildings in Oxford are named after him, including the John Radcliffe Hospital. The Radcliffe Library in Oxford was founded by his will as was the Radcliffe Trust, one of Britain's oldest charities, supporting music, heritage and crafts[xvi].

This plaque was funded by a National Lottery Grant.

43 The Rotary Club of Wakefield

◉ Strafford Arms, Bull Ring

The Rotary Club of Wakefield celebrated its 100th anniversary in 2021 and we were approached to see if a blue plaque could be erected to mark the Club's first meeting which had taken place at the Strafford Ams Hotel on 3rd June 1921.

The Strafford Arms Hotel of 1921 is no more, having been demolished in the 1960s and replaced on the same site with the modern building you see today.

This plaque was funded by The Rotary Club of Wakefield.

2021: Rotary President Stuart Livesey with the author

44 William Whiteley

📍 **Central Chambers, The Bull Ring**

William Whiteley (1831-1907) dubbed the 'Universal Provider' learned his trade as a shopkeeper in the premises near here of Harnew and Glover, drapers, where he was apprenticed in 1848.

As a boy he lived at Agbrigg. On completing his apprenticeship, he left Wakefield in 1855, and apparently inspired by what he had seen at the Great Exhibition at Crystal Palace in 1851, Whiteley moved to London where he set up a fancy goods shop, opening in 1863. He went on to found one of the world's first department stores in Bayswater.

Whiteley was shot and killed in his store in 1907 by a deranged man, 29-year-old Horace Rayner, who claimed to be his illegitimate son, something which was never proved but, after his death, a number of Whiteley's extra-marital affairs came to light.

Rayner was sentenced to 12 years in prison. In the meantime, the business continued under the management of Whiteley's two sons, re-locating to new premises on Queensway in 1911. The store was eventually taken over by Selfridges in 1927 but ceased to trade as a department store in 1981[xvii]. At the time of writing, the building is being converted into private residences, restaurants, bars, and retail[xviii].

This plaque was funded by a National Lottery grant.

45 John Potter

📍 **Black Rock, Cross Square**

Wakefield can boast two archbishops, one of Canterbury and the other of York, as her sons. The second is the former Archbishop of York, the Most Reverend Dr David Hope (born 1940). The earlier one was Archbishop John Potter (1674-1747) who succeeded to the see of Canterbury in 1737. He lived here as a boy above his father's draper's shop (the building we see today would not become a pub until the 1840s) and attended Queen Elizabeth Grammar School and then University College, Oxford.

This plaque was funded by a National Lottery grant.

46 Noel Gay

WAKEFIELD CIVIC SOCIETY

NOEL GAY (1898-1954), LYRICIST AND POPULAR-SONG WRITER AND COMPOSER OF THE "LAMBETH WALK" WAS A CHORISTER AT WAKEFIELD CATHEDRAL IN HIS TEENAGE YEARS.

2005

Wakefield Cathedral, Northgate

Noel Gay (1898-1954), born Reginald Armitage, best known as a lyricist and popular-song writer. His early training was as a chorister at the Cathedral. At the age of fifteen he won a scholarship from Queen Elizabeth Grammar School to the Royal College of Music in London and became assistant organist at the Chapel Royal, St James' Palace. Later, at Cambridge, he discovered his talent for popular songs.

He wrote the music, and sometimes the words, for a number of revues and musical comedies, including the 1937 musical, *Me and My Girl*, which includes his *The Lambeth Walk*.

He is said to have adopted the names of actor and playwright Noel Coward and actress and singer Maisie Gay, whose names he had seen on a bill poster for a show in which they were both appearing. He also wrote under the pseudonym Stanley Hill.

This plaque was part-funded by a contribution from Wakefield Grammar School Foundation.

47 Manor House Yard

WAKEFIELD CIVIC SOCIETY

RECORDS

HERE WAS MANOR HOUSE YARD IN WHICH STOOD THE MANOR HOUSE INN, THE MOOT HALL AND THE ROLLS OFFICE OF THE VAST MANOR OF WAKEFIELD.

2000

Upper Kirkgate

Sited on the front of Boot's, the plaque here commemorates Manor House Yard and the Moot Hall and Rolls Office of the great Manor of Wakefield which were both in the yard. The Manor, created in medieval times, stretched from Normanton in the east to Todmorden in the West. Its courts were peripatetic but in Wakefield meetings were held in the Moot Hall. The records of the courts were held in the Rolls Office.

Since Norman times, the Manor was governed from Sandal Castle where the Steward of the Manor lived.

However, with the rebuilding of the Moot Hall in upper Kirkgate in the first half of the 16th century (during the reign of Henry VIII) as a place for the Steward of the Manor to live, and the building of a new prison in Wakefield in the 1590s, administrative matters moved away from the castle and into the town centre.

The Moot Hall was demolished in 1913 but would have stood behind where Boot's stands today.

This plaque was funded by a Millennium Lottery grant.

48 Arthur Greenwood

Blue plaque text:
WAKEFIELD CIVIC SOCIETY
ARTHUR GREENWOOD
(1880-1954)
MEMBER OF PARLIAMENT FOR WAKEFIELD 1932-1954 AND A CABINET MEMBER DURING WORLD WAR II.
AS CHAIRMAN OF THE CABINET SOCIAL SERVICES COMMITTEE, HE WAS INSTRUMENTAL IN FOUNDING THE NATIONAL HEALTH SERVICE AND THE NATIONAL INSURANCE SCHEME
2013

📍 **Greenwood House, George Street**

Arthur Greenwood (1880-1954) was born in Hunslet, Leeds, the son of William Greenwood, a painter and decorator, and Margaret Greenwood (née Nunns).

He was first elected as an MP in the 1922 general election where he stood as the Labour candidate for Nelson and Colne in Lancashire, a seat he held until the general election in 1931. In 1932, he stood as the Labour candidate for Wakefield in a bye-election and was successful, holding the seat until his death in 1954. His constituency office was on George Street.

Greenwood was made Deputy Leader of the party under Clement Atlee and served in Churchill's War Cabinet as Minister without Portfolio when the wartime coalition government was formed.

From 1942 until the end of the war, he served as Leader of the Opposition in the House as Atlee was in the Coalition Cabinet.

His responsibilities to prepare the country for the post-war recovery led to the creation of the NHS and the National Insurance Scheme.

This plaque was funded by donations from a number of individuals including former Labour Councillor and Mayor of Wakefield David Atkinson, former MP for Wakefield David Hinchliffe, and the then MP for Wakefield Mary Creagh. The local Labour Party also made a contribution.

49 Dr Crowther's Almshouses

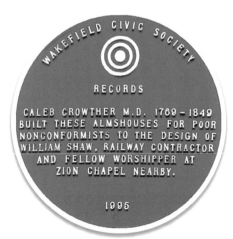

Blue plaque text:
WAKEFIELD CIVIC SOCIETY
RECORDS
CALEB CROWTHER M.D. 1769-1849 BUILT THESE ALMSHOUSES FOR POOR NONCONFORMISTS TO THE DESIGN OF WILLIAM SHAW, RAILWAY CONTRACTOR AND FELLOW WORSHIPPER AT ZION CHAPEL NEARBY.
1995

📍 **George Street**

Caleb Crowther was physician to the Wakefield Dispensary (the forerunner of Clayton Hospital). In 1838 he bought land in George Street as the site of future almshouses. He died in 1848 leaving provision in his will for the almhouses. They were built to a design by William Shaw (see entry No. 12) and opened in 1863.

Crowther himself is buried at the rear of the property. The almshouses are managed today by the Wakefield Grammar School Foundation.

This plaque was funded by a National Lottery grant. It was refurbished in 2023 with the Society meeting the cost.

50 Cattle Market

Royal Mail Sorting Office, Market Street

The plaque here marks the site of the Wakefield Cattle Market which opened in 1765 and was one of the largest in the north of England. Drovers brought livestock long distances by road and the animals were then pastured in fields on the outskirts of the town to await sale. Three local public houses had the name The Graziers for this reason, one of them overlooking the Cattle Market itself. (Today, only one, on Aberford Road in Stanley, remains in use as a pub).

The cattle were sold in the Market Place (now the Bull Ring) and at the top of Westgate until the dedicated cattle market was created in the aptly named Market Street.

The market, initially held fortnightly but then weekly from 1849, became the largest in England and continued to operate until 1963.

With the coming of the railways, livestock could be brought to Wakefield by train, but the animals were still walked to the market from the stations at Kirkgate and Westgate.

This plaque was funded by a Millennium Lottery grant.

51 Denby Dale Turnpike

Sainsbury's, Corner of Ings Road and Denby Dale Road

In medieval times, responsibility for maintaining roads usually fell to the parish, or the Lord of the Manor who would require his tenants to provide their labour. However, this resulted in roads of different repair quality and people living in areas with lots of through traffic felt an unfair burden was imposed on them. As more people travelled, and travelled long distances, the arrangement proved unsatisfactory. The problem was recognised when, in 1663, Parliament passed the first of the Turnpike Acts authorising the creation of trusts that could levy tolls on road users to repair and improve the road.

The trusts were not-for-profit and maximum toll limits were set.

Here the Ings turnpike (1831-1863) meets the Denby Dale turnpike (1825-1874). Both were new roads, the latter being by far the more useful and popular. Although Ings Road was intended as a quick route from Wakefield Bridge for traffic going west, the tolls made it unpopular and the preferred route remained going via Kirkgate and Westgate.

This plaque was funded by a National Lottery grant.

52 Isaak Donner and the Wakefield Shirt Company

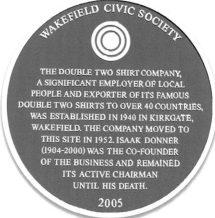

Thornes Lane Wharf

The Wakefield Shirt Company was founded in 1940 by Isaak Donner (1904-2000), a refugee from the Nazi occupation, and his partner Frank Myers in premises on the corner of Kirkgate and George Street. Here the famous Double Two Shirts were manufactured, developing a concept which had been founded when Donner's father was in business in Vienna.

The patented shirts were designed to allow for the collar to be easily replaced when it showed signs of wear. Each new shirt came with a replacement collar which could easily be sewn into the place of the removed collar.

The new product was an instant success and as the shirts had two collars and in some cases two sets of cuffs, the shirts were called Double TWO shirts. The innovation became so successful that the company came to be known by the name of the shirts[xix].

The company prospered and in 1952 moved to a much larger site at Portobello Mills. Although the company has diversified, into making industrial workwear and professional uniforms, for example, it is still a family-run business.

This plaque was funded by the Wakefield Shirt Company Ltd.

53 William (Bill) Alfred Ismay

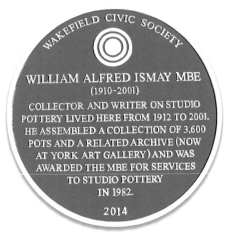

14 Welbeck Street, Barnsley Road

William Alfred Ismay MBE (1910-2001) was the most prolific collector of British Studio pottery in the post-war period. During his lifetime, his collection of over 3600 pots and related archives of 10,000+ items was stacked and stored on every available surface in the house where he lived from the age of 18 months until his death.

Born in Wakefield and educated at Wakefield Grammar School and Leeds University, where he studied Classics, Ismay became a librarian and ended up as Head Librarian at the Hemsworth Library before retiring in 1975 but used his limited financial resources to build his collection, starting in the 1950s.

As well as purchasing pieces by established makers, he also sought out new potters to support them by purchasing samples of their work early in their careers and over 500 makers are represented in the collection. Ismay wrote about pottery and ceramics and was a founder member of the Northern Potters Association. He was awarded the MBE for services to studio pottery in the New Year's Honours list for 1982.

Ismay bequeathed his collection to the Yorkshire Museum and it is now in the care of York Museums Trust.

This plaque was funded with donations from the Northern Potters Association and the York Museums Trust.

54 The Dunkirk Connection

ON SATURDAY 8TH JUNE 1940, 3RD BATTALION GRENADIER GUARDS MUSTERED BEHIND THIS CHURCH TO COUNT THOSE KILLED AND MISSING DURING THE WITHDRAWAL TO DUNKIRK. ON SUNDAY THE BATTALION RETURNED TO WORSHIP IN ST. HELEN'S. WAKEFIELD'S HOSPITALITY HELPED RESTORE SPIRITS FOR SUBSEQUENT ACTIONS IN NORTH AFRICA AND ITALY. 2017

📍 **St Helen's Church, Barnsley Road, Sandal**

And so we come to the only blue plaque in our collection (so far) that isn't actually blue.

At the end of 2016, the Society was contacted by former Wakefield resident Gerry Southworth. As a young boy, he was witness to an event that happened in 1940 and which he felt merited a plaque.

Following the withdrawal of Allied troops from the beaches of Dunkirk in World War II under 'Operation Dynamo', which started towards the end of May and ended on 4th June 1940, evacuated personnel were dispersed around the country to receive hospital treatment where required, or just to recuperate and regroup.

A train brought members of the 3rd Battalion Grenadier Guards to Wakefield, arriving here on 4th June. They were billeted wherever accommodation could be found for them – church and village halls and in the homes of Wakefield residents. Some were taken to Pinderfields Hospital for treatment. On 8th June, surviving members of the Battalion were mustered in the grounds of St Helen's Church. The following day, they returned to the Church for a service and a parade, which Gerry saw.

The plaque nomination was agreed along with a request from the Vicar that the plaque be in a colour sympathetic to the colour of the stone in which the church was built.

This plaque was funded by the Grenadier Guards.

55 John Nevison

JOHN NEVISON (1639-1685), THE FAMOUS ROBBER AND HIGHWAYMAN, SEEN BY SOME AS A LATTER-DAY ROBIN HOOD, WAS REPUTEDLY ARRESTED IN THE THREE HOUSES INN AT SANDAL PRIOR TO HIS CONVICTION AND EXECUTION AT YORK IN 1685. 2009

📍 **Three Houses Inn, Barnsley Road, Sandal**

17th century Highwayman John Nevison, who is thought to have come originally from Wortley, near Barnsley, and to have served under the Duke of York in Flanders, was allegedly arrested while sleeping in a chair at the Magpie, one of three inns (the Raven, the Plough and the Magpie) that stood next to each other on Barnsley Road at Sandal. (The name 'Three Houses' seems to have been coined later). He was later hanged at York Castle in 1685 (some sources give 1684 or other dates).

It was on his return to England that Nevison entered into his nefarious ways, earning the nickname 'Swift Nick' – said to have been given him by King Charles II after a 200-mile dash on horseback that Nevison made from Kent to York to establish an alibi for a robbery he had committed earlier the same day. During his career as a highwayman, he was arrested a number of times but managed to escape each time until his final arrest at Sandal.

This plaque was funded by the then owners of the Three Houses Inn in 2009.

56 East Lodge

East Lodge

WAKEFIELD CIVIC SOCIETY

EAST LODGE

This is one of nine lodges built around 1870 by Sir Lionel Milborne-Swinnerton-Pilkington, (1835-1901) 11th baronet of Chevet Hall (now demolished).

Strategically placed, the lodge housed estate workers who were employed to protect the game and restrict public access to the park.

2016

📍 **Newmillerdam**

Sir Lionel Milborne-Swinnerton-Pilkington (1835-1901) was the 11th Baronet of the Pilkington Baronetcy of Stanley. The Baronetcy was created in 1635 for Arthur Pilkington along with 6,000 acres of land in Nova Scotia. The fifth Baronet, Sir Lionel Pilkington, (c.1707-1778) was a British Member of Parliament. He purchased Chevet Hall (demolished in 1955) as the family home.

The 11th Baronet, appears to have been born at Chevet Hall in 1835. During his lifetime, he was responsible for building at least nine lodges around the estate. The lodges housed estate workers such as agricultural labourers, coachmen and gardeners.

In 2015, Wakefield Civic Society member Gill Sykes, chair of the Newmillerdam Liaison Group, proposed a blue plaque for the East Lodge, on the footpath leading along the east side of the lake towards the boathouse. There was a plan to convert the lodge into a community hub and Gill offered to raise funds for the plaque. The plaque was unveiled in 2016 but the start of the project was delayed and the plaque has still to be fixed in place at the time of writing.

For interest, the West Lodge, on the other side of the lake, has for some years operated as an Italian restaurant, La Fortezza.

This plaque was funded by monies raised by Gill Sykes (see photo on page 5).

57 Aire and Calder Navigation

WAKEFIELD CIVIC SOCIETY

RECORDS

UNTIL 1850 THIS BUILDING HOUSED THE BOARDROOM OF THE AIRE AND CALDER NAVIGATION, A WATERWAYS COMPANY ESTABLISHED IN 1699 AND FOR LONG BRITAINS RICHEST.

2000

📍 **Navigation Yard, near Wakefield Bridge**

In the 18th century, Wakefield was, in effect, an inland port and sea-going vessels were built and repaired here. This was made possible because of the new canals, or navigations, that were being cut.

The Rivers Aire and Calder were made navigable to Leeds and Wakefield about 1702, and both towns then became thriving inland ports. The body responsible for the necessary dredging, construction of locks, etc, was the Aire and Calder Navigation.

Here, at what was the head of the navigable waterway in Wakefield, the company built its offices and boardroom.

Until the coming of railways, the company saw vast traffic on its waterways and made immense profits for its shareholders, at one time paying a dividend of 200%. As the navigable route from Wakefield was extended westwards by the Calder and Hebble Navigation, traffic became even more extensive.

This plaque was funded by a Millennium Lottery grant.

58 Joseph Rhodes

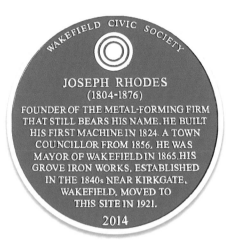

Group Rhodes, Caldervale Road

Joseph Rhodes (1804-1876) made machines that enabled others to do or make things. He made his first machine in a small workshop in 1824 but, in the 1840s, he established the Grove Iron Works, at the bottom of Kirkgate near to where the Eastwood building stands today.

In the 1920s, the company expanded and moved into larger premises at Belle Vue. Over the years, a series of acquisitions, mergers and takeovers has created a large company, Group Rhodes, one of Europe's largest Original Equipment Manufacturers in its field.

The main divisions of the Group consist of Joseph Rhodes, Rhodes Interform, Craven Fawcett, Beauford Engineers, Rhodes Environmental, Slater & Crabtree and Hallamshire Engineering[xx].

As well as his business interests, Joseph Rhodes served as a town councillor from 1856 and was the Mayor of Wakefield in 1865.

When the company closed the Belle Vue site, the plaque was moved to their headquarter offices on Calder Vale Road.

This plaque was funded by Group Rhodes.

59 Richmal Mangnall

Crofton Academy, High Street, Crofton

Richmal Mangnall (1769-1820) was first a pupil, then a teacher and then the head teacher at Crofton Hall School, a private boarding school for young ladies established in Crofton Old Hall (built circa 1750 and demolished in the 1870s, to be replaced by a new Hall – now part of Crofton Academy).

Mangnall wrote three books: *Historical and Miscellaneous Questions For the Use of Young People* (1798); *Half an Hour's Lounge,* or *Poems* (1805); and *Compendium of Geography* (1815). The first of these, known more informally as 'Mangnall's Questions' was used to teach children and its popularity as a teaching aid among teachers and governesses led to it staying in print long after her death.

Miss Mangnall died on May Day 1820 and is buried in Crofton Churchyard. Among the pupils she taught were Maria and Elizabeth Brontë, older sisters to Charlotte, Emily and Anne[xxi].

This plaque was funded by Crofton History Group with additional donations from Constable's and Pinder's Charity, Crofton Smoke Signal, and Crofton Parish Council.

60 Trevor Hatherton

45 Long Row, New Sharlston

Trevor Hatherton was born at 12, Long Row, New Sharlston on 30th September 1924. His parents were Baden Hector Hatherton a coal hewer and Evelyn Hatherton (née Burrough). He was educated at Lee Brigg Primary School and Normanton Grammar School. From these relatively humble beginnings, he went on to University in Birmingham and London, before taking a job as a geophysicist in New Zealand.

From there, he explored the Antarctic (on foot), being awarded the Antarctic Medal (as were Scott and Shackleton). He became the Chief Scientist at Scott Base on Antarctica and eventually had a glacier and the laboratories at the base named after him.

He was awarded an OBE in 1958 and was President of the Royal Society of New Zealand 1985-89.

Hatherton died in 1992 and that might have been the end of the story. However, Richard Burrough, whose father was Hatherton's cousin, had been researching his family tree and discovered the details of Hatherton's life and achievements and proposed him for a blue plaque. Members of the Hatherton family from around the world gathered in Wakefield for the unveiling, including Hatherton's daughter Kate, who had flown over with her husband Garth who was then President of the Royal Society of New Zealand.

Richard Burrough organised funding for the plaque securing donations from family members.

61 Kirkgate Station

Monk Street

At one time, Primrose Hill was cultivated as strawberry fields and gardens. These gave way to the Portland Cement works of Leeds businessman Joseph Aspdin in 1825. The cement works relocated to Ings Road when the railway came through.

Kirkgate Station first opened in 1840 as 'Wakefield' station on a route being built by the Manchester and Leeds Railway (the Lancashire & Yorkshire Railway from 1846). In 1872, the station was restyled as Wakefield Kirkgate. When first built, the passenger facilities were no more than wooden huts but the station was rebuilt in the Italianate style in 1854.

Sadly, the station fell into decline even though still in use for passenger services and attracted the attention of national media and politicians including Lord Adonis, Secretary of State for Transport. In 2014, the station underwent significant refurbishment by Groundwork who then moved into the building and commissioned a blue plaque from the Society. The plaque was made up but a change in personnel and internal re-organisation within Groundwork meant that the plaque was not erected. At the time of writing, efforts are being made to see that the plaque does indeed go up on the station.

This plaque was funded by Groundwork Wakefield.

5.   Making a Blue Plaque Nomination

As you might imagine, we regularly receive nominations for additional plaques to add to our collection and we are keen to encourage these.

However, we do have a process that we follow on the receipt of a nomination and not all nominations will result in a new plaque. When a nomination is agreed, the minimum period we need to commission and take delivery of a new plaque is around 6–8 weeks, but it can take longer, and there are several things that need to happen.

We can only consider nominations for the Society's 'area of benefit' – the geographical area covered by the Society as a registered charity. This includes the city of Wakefield and surrounding areas but not other towns in the Metropolitan District. (There is a map of our 'area of benefit' on our website. See: wakefieldcivicsociety.org.uk/our-area-of-benefit)

When commemorating a person, plaques are only erected posthumously and we would usually allow a gap of at least 20 years after someone's death before considering a plaque.

The Blue Plaque Process

1. Nominations

Nominations can be made by post (to *Wakefield Civic Society, PO Box 380, Wakefield, WF1 3WT*) or email (to info@wakefieldcivicsocety.org.uk). You can use our nomination form if you wish.

When a new nomination is received, we will ask whoever is making the nomination to provide as much factual background information as possible to help the Society's committee to reach a decision on the suitability or otherwise of the person, building or event being nominated. If the nomination is for a person, the Society will look for evidence of 'worthiness' and a connection to Wakefield. The person need not have been born in Wakefield but should have spent some part of their life in the area or have performed some significant act worthy of commemoration while visiting the city. We will look for facts to support the nomination and want to know why the person is judged worthy of nomination.

Nominations for a building or event will be subjected to similar scrutiny to ascertain the local, regional and/or national interest.

2. Location, location, location

We will need to find somewhere for the plaque to go.

If the plaque is to commemorate the life of an individual, we would ideally like to find a building that has a close association with the individual being nominated – for example, a building in which the individual lived or worked (or was born/died). Sometimes, the original building may have been demolished and a new building erected on the site and sometimes the original building may have been demolished and not replaced – it might, for example, have been demolished to allow for a new road or similar development. Where there is no obvious building, we will need to see if there is another building that would be an appropriate location for the plaque but if there is no suitable location, the nomination may fail at this point.

If the nomination is for a building, priority will be given to nominations for buildings with interesting histories that help to tell the story of Wakefield and its development.

There are a number of things to consider in choosing a location for a plaque:

- Is there already a blue plaque on the building? We usually aim to put just one plaque on any building but there are exceptions where two plaques might be agreed.

- Is there a more worthy or suitable nomination for the building being considered? As already mentioned, the Society has a long list of nominations and it may be that the building someone wishes to nominate a plaque for has already been nominated, or that there is more than one person associated with a given building. The Society would use its own discretion in deciding which plaque nomination to take forward for any given location.

- Is there somewhere on the building to which a plaque can be affixed? Sometimes, because of decorative embellishments or the position of windows and doors, there may not be a satisfactory position on the building to affix a plaque. Where possible, we do prefer to lift plaques higher up the elevation of a building so that they cannot easily be tampered with and to prevent accidental damage.

3. Permissions

Before we can proceed with a blue plaque, we will need to sort out some permissions.

The first of these will be permission from the owner of the property. Sometimes, this is not the person or business that is occupying the property. If a building is tenanted, we will need to find out who the actual owner is and it may be possible that the terms of any tenancy agreement will require both the owner and tenant to agree. Agreement will then also need to be reached on exactly where the plaque should go on the building.

Listed building consent: If the building identified for a new plaque is listed, we will need to liaise with the Council over obtaining listed building consent. This can take up to 12 weeks.

Family: Where the person being nominated has close surviving family members, we may need to seek their agreement to a plaque.

Wording: We will need to agree the exact form of the wording on the blue plaque with all parties.

4. Funding

The Society will need funds to pay for each new plaque

At the time of writing, a new plaque will cost something in the region of £700–£750. This includes VAT and delivery but the exact price will depend on the size of the plaque (usually 18 to 20 inches in diameter) and the amount of text – the more words, the higher the cost. As a small charity, the Society cannot afford to pay for all the blue plaques for which we receive nominations, so we always seek donations to cover the cost. If you are putting forward a nomination, we will ask you to cover the cost of the plaque or to help us to find the funding from other sources. No plaque can be ordered until the Society has received the funding in advance.

6. Wakefield Civic Society

Wakefield Civic Society: An organisation dedicated to making Wakefield a better place in which to live, work or relax.

Whether you are a resident or a visitor to Wakefield, the Society can offer something of interest. We run a full programme of events throughout the year. Many of our talks are now recorded and can be watched on our Vimeo page – vimeo.com/wakefieldcivicsociety.

Our members receive regular updates on what is happening in Wakefield and have opportunities to take part in the debate on how Wakefield develops. The Society was established in 1964 out of a concern for the built environment of our city. As a registered charity (number 236034), the Society is dedicated both to preserving and celebrating our built heritage and to campaigning for new developments to be of the very highest standard and quality possible. We regularly scrutinise planning applications submitted to the council and raise comments where we consider it appropriate to do so. We also discuss proposals for new developments with property owners, developers and council officials in order to help improve outcomes.

We run an annual design and environmental awards scheme where we recognise the very best in architectural and environmental projects to promote an interest in and awareness of the importance of good design and care for the environment.

As a charity, the Society depends principally for its income on the annual subscriptions it receives from its members and on donations received from members of the public and we offer a range of personal and corporate memberships. To find out more about the work of the Society and how you can help us, please visit our website www.wakefieldcivicsociety.org.uk or follow us on Twitter/X @WakefieldCivicS.

The Society is run by a committee of elected volunteers who receive no remuneration for their work. All proceeds from the sale of this publication go to support the work of the Society.

'Building interest in Wakefield since 1964'

7. Notes and Further Reading

i   Wilkinson, John F, *For Grammar and Other Good learning: Glimpses into the History of Queen Elizabeth Grammar School, Wakefield*, The Governors of Wakefield Grammar School Foundation 1991

ii   Taylor, Kate (Ed), *Worthies of Wakefield*, Wakefield Historical Publications, 2004

iii See: engole.info/potovens-pottery

iv   Hallett, Christine, *Nurses of Passchendale*, Pen and Sword History, 2017

v   See: en.wikipedia.org/wiki/Lake_Lock_Rail_Road

vi   George, Nora, J., *Sir Alec Clegg: Practical Idealist 1909-1986*, Wharncliffe Books, 2000

vii Wolfenden, John, *The Memoirs of Lord Wolfenden*, The Bodley Head, 1976

viii Forrester, Heather, *The Other Percy Metcalfe, Edition 49, The Medal Magazine*, Autumn 2006

ix   Trickett, Kevin, *Westgate Wakefield*, Wakefield Civic Society, 2022

x   Trickett, Kevin., Ibid

xi   Dawson, Paul, *Wakefield at Work*, Amberley Publishing, 2020

xii Scriven, David, *Pemberton House 122 Westgate*, Wakefield Historical Society 2022

xiii See: institutionalhistory.com/homepage/prisons/major-prisons/wakefield-prison

xiv Smith, Linda, *65 Westgate*, Wakefield Historical Society, 2022

xv   Taylor, Kate, *The Making of Wakefield 1801-1900*, Wharncliffe Books, 2008

xvi See: theradcliffetrust.org

xvii Boase, Tessa, *London's Lost Department Stores*, Safe Haven Books Ltd, 2022

xviii See: www.thewhiteleylondon.com

xix www.doubletwo.co.uk/our-shirt-making-heritage

xx   www.grouprhodes.co.uk

xxi See: magnall.net/km-1750-1774/km032-richmal-mangnall

8. Acknowledgements

Blue Plaque Photos

When blue plaques are first delivered, they are rather shiny and reflective – which makes photography rather difficult as they tend to reflect the photographer. After a period of being exposed to the elements, the shininess dissipates but by then the plaques are affixed to a wall, possibly 10 feet off the ground – which makes photography equally difficult. On top of this, different light conditions can render photographs of our blue plaques in slightly different shades of blue – even though they all come from the manufacturer in a standard hue. One further complication is that, when our first blue plaques went up in 1995 and 2000, no one took individual photographs of the plaques.

As a result of the above, although we do now have photos for all our plaques, they come in various shades and some of the older plaques were looking rather tired (we are in the process of refurbishing those that need attention). For this book, I wanted images of the plaques that were consistent and I am grateful to Wakefield Civic Society Executive Committee member Vicky Flintoff who has assiduously worked her way through over 60 photographs to ensure that the ones reproduced in this book all match.

Design

The layout of this book was designed by Wakefield-based design agency Rhubarb Design House, a corporate member of the Society (see: rhubarbdesignhouse.uk)

Thank You

As well as acknowledging all the individuals and organisations who contributed to the cost of our blue plaques, the Society also wishes to place on record its appreciation to the many property owners and tenants for giving their consent to us putting up a plaque on their buildings.

In terms of this book, we are grateful to Wakefield Council for the award of a Culture Grant as part of Our Year – Wakefield District 2024 to cover the cost of design and print.

About the Author

Kevin Trickett MBE, BA (Hons), MBA, MA (Phil)

After a 40-year career in the Civil Service, Kevin now devotes much of his time to charity work, writing, public speaking, and travel.

Kevin writes and speaks about some of his favourite subjects including architecture, heritage, travel and Art Deco.

Kevin is well-versed in the activities of the civic movement, having been a trustee of Wakefield Civic Society since 1990. He was elected as the Society's President in March 2002 and continues to hold that position today.

Shortly after taking up the presidency of Wakefield Civic Society, he became a trustee of the Yorkshire and Humber Association of Civic Societies (YHACS) and was elected as its Chair in January 2011, a role which he also continues to fulfil at the time of writing.

Kevin was a trustee of the national charity Civic Trust from 2004 to 2009 where, amongst other responsibilities, he chaired the National Committee for Civic Societies.

After the demise of the Civic Trust, Kevin worked to help set up Civic Voice, a new national body for civic and amenity societies, which was established in 2010.

Kevin's other voluntary work includes his former role as Deputy Chair of arts charity Beam. He also did a seven-year stint as a trustee of the Community Foundation for Wakefield. He currently serves as a member of the Creative Wakefield Board and represents Wakefield Civic Society on the Wakefield High Street Task Force.

You will often see Kevin leading guided walks around Wakefield on behalf of the Civic Society and you might encounter him giving one of his talks about the work of the Society to community groups.

In the 2018 New Year's Honours List, Kevin was awarded an MBE for services to the community in Wakefield.

 You can follow Kevin on Twitter/X: @MrTrickett